P9-BYN-704

PRIMARY SOURCES OF
FAMOUS PEOPLE IN AMERICAN HISTORY™

CRISPUS ATTUCKS

HERO OF THE BOSTON MASSACRE

ANNE BEIER

rosen central
Primary Source™

The Rosen Publishing Group, Inc., New York

To Christopher W. Douglass, and in memory of Warner Feig

Published in 2004 by The Rosen Publishing Group, Inc.
29 East 21st Street, New York, NY 10010

Library of Congress Cataloging-in-Publication Data

Beier, Anne.
Crispus Attucks : hero of the Boston Massacre / by Anne Beier.
  p. cm. — (Primary Sources of Famous people in American history)
Summary: Introduces the life of Crispus Attucks, a former slave who died in the Boston Massacre, a fight between the British and American colonists that occurred before the American Revolution.
Includes bibliographical references and index.
ISBN 0-8239-4106-X (library binding)
ISBN 0-8239-4178-7 (pbk.)
6-pack ISBN 0-8239-4305-4
1. Attucks, Crispus, d. 1770—Juvenile literature. 2. Boston Massacre, 1770—Juvenile literature. 3. African Americans—Biography—Juvenile literature. [1. Attucks, Crispus, d. 1770. 2. Boston Massacre, 1770. 3. African Americans—Biography.]
I. Title. II. Series.
E185.97.A86 B45 2003
973.3'113'092—dc21

2002155940

Manufactured in the United States of America

Photo credits: cover, pp. 5, 21, 23, 29 © Hulton/Archive/Getty Images; p. 7 The New-York Historical Society, New York, USA/The Bridgeman Art Library; p. 8 The Mariners' Museum, Newport News, VA; p. 9 Christie's Images/The Bridgeman Art Library; p. 10 Smithsonian American Art Museum, Washington, DC/Art Resource, NY; pp. 11, 24, 25 © North Wind Picture Archives; p. 13 Yale University Art Gallery, New Haven, CT/The Bridgeman Art Library; p. 14 Eastman Johnson, *A Ride for Liberty—The Fugitive Slaves,* 1863, Collection of the Brooklyn Museum of Art, 40.59a; pp. 15, 26, 27 Picture Collection, The Branch Libraries, The New York Public Library, Astor, Lenox, and Tilden Foundations; p. 17 Archives Charmet/The Bridgeman Art Library; p. 19 Bonhams, London, UK/The Bridgeman Art Library; p. 20 Réunion des Musées Nationaux/Art Resource, NY; p. 22 © Corbis.

Designer: Thomas Forget; Photo Researcher: Rebecca Anguin-Cohen

CONTENTS

1 A YOUNG LAD WITH BIG DREAMS

In 1723, Crispus Attucks was born into slavery in Framingham, Massachusetts. His father, Prince, was captured in Africa. He was brought to the colonies and sold as a slave. Nancy, Crispus's mother, was a member of the Natick Indian tribe. Crispus had an older sister, Phebe. The family served their master, Colonel Buckminster.

THE NATIVE INDIANS

The Natick Praying Indian tribe still remains in Natick, Massachusetts. Nancy, Crispus's mother, belonged to this tribe. It is a small tribe. The year 2002 marked its 350th anniversary.

This drawing of Crispus Attucks is one of the few that exist. Crispus wanted to be free from slavery from a young age.

In his early teens, Crispus wanted to be free. He did not like the idea of being owned. Attucks dreamed of becoming a sailor. Colonel Buckminster had no ships. Later, Attucks was sold to a new master, William Brown. Crispus was forced to move to Boston near the shipping docks.

DID YOU KNOW?

The word "attucks" is a Natick Indian word. It means a small, male deer. It was considered a good name for a strong person.

Shown above is a view of Boston Harbor around 1800. Ships from Europe sailed into the harbor every week. Whaling ships used men from the Boston area as sailors.

William Brown taught Crispus the cattle business. He bought and sold cattle for his master. Crispus became very good at his new trade. His dreams of becoming a free man had not died. Attucks did not like that dark-skinned people were forced into slavery. He wanted to escape slavery and become a sailor.

Sailors in the mid-1700s wore a simple uniform. A warm jacket helped in the cold of the North Atlantic. Hats were important for protection against the harsh sun.

Crispus Attucks kept extra money he made from selling cows. He saved his money. He wanted to buy his freedom. But his master did not want to let him free.

2 ATTUCKS MAKES A PLAN

Crispus watched the ships that always returned to the harbor. Soon he was able to spot a stray ship. It was a whaling ship. One night William Brown was away. Crispus slipped away to talk to the captain. The captain liked that Crispus was a big, strong man. Crispus was also known to be tough and a fighter.

Crispus was known around Boston. He had friends who were sailors. Ship captains were often looking for new sailors. Crispus used this information to plan his escape.

Whaling ships captured whales for their blubber (fat). Oil is left after boiling away the water in blubber. This oil was used for candles and lamps.

The captain hired him that night. Crispus went below deck to hide. He worried that he might be captured before the ship left port. The ship sailed out to sea the next morning. Crispus was happy that his dreams were coming true.

DID YOU KNOW?

Crispus used other names after he ran away so he would not be caught. After a few years, people gave up trying to find him.

Whaling sailors did not use the ship to capture whales. A group of men set out in a large rowboat. One man stood at the front of the boat with a harpoon (spear).

Soon after, William Brown discovered that Crispus had run away. On October 2, 1750, Brown placed an announcement in the *Boston Gazette*. It stated that Crispus Attucks was a runaway slave. From then on, Crispus always had to be careful. If he was caught, he would lose his newfound freedom.

Crispus Attucks was not the only slave who dreamed of freedom. Slaves often ran away from mean masters. Many runaway slaves were caught.

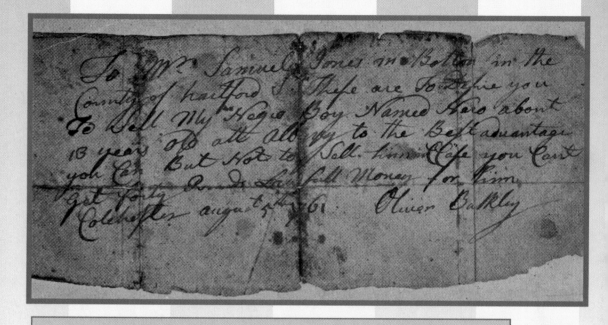

Owners sold slaves any way they could. This bill of sale shows
how easily slave families could be broken apart.

3 TWENTY YEARS AT SEA

For the next twenty years, Crispus worked on ships at sea. He learned to hunt and catch whales. Work on whaling ships was dangerous.

Crispus learned to throw a harpoon. In those days, whales were worth a lot of money. Whale blubber was turned into oil for burning in lamps.

CRISPUS ON BOARD SHIP

Crispus started as a seaman on his first whaling ship. Over time, he became a skilled harpooner. This job was the most difficult. He would have only a few chances to throw harpoons to kill a whale.

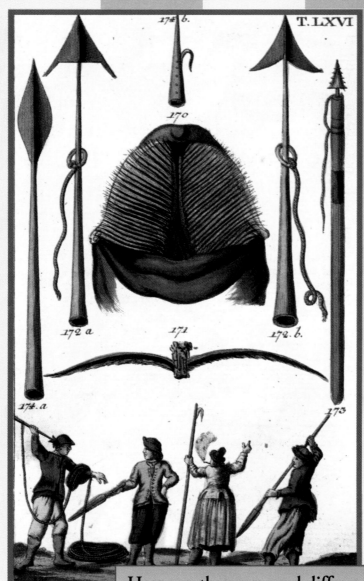

Harpoon throwers used different kinds of tips. Some were long and narrow. Others had wide heads.

17

Whaling captains valued Crispus's hard work and courage. As a harpooner, he earned good wages. Crispus missed his family, though. He was at sea most of the year. Sometimes the ship returned to Boston. At these times, Crispus secretly visited his family. Luckily, he was never caught.

DANGERS AT SEA

Life at sea was full of hardships. Seamen had to outlast bad storms. There was always fear of attacks from pirates and British ships.

Whaling was a hard job. Whales were much larger than the boats. Sometimes the whale would overturn the boat.

4 TOUGH TIMES FOR THE AMERICAN COLONIES

In the 1770s, American colonists wanted independence from Great Britain. King George of England did not like this idea. He sent British soldiers to control the colonists. King George placed high taxes on goods sent to the colonies. This angered the colonists. Life became uneasy between the British and the colonists.

King George III of Britain placed heavy taxes on many goods. Americans needed to buy these goods to live.

People in all the colonies spoke out against high taxes. They had no rights that could help them fight these taxes. American colonists began to fight for freedom.

Crispus continued to work on whalers during the 1770s. He often heard about the trouble in the colonies. He understood their strong need for independence. He had been working and hiding for his own freedom. Crispus wanted to help the colonists' cause. He feared being captured and returned to slavery, though.

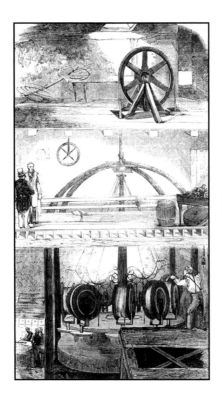

When Crispus was not at sea, he worked as a ropemaker. Small factories in Boston made rope for whaling ships.

Colonial political leaders began to meet in each
colony. They wrote letters to King George to tell him
of their anger. King George ignored these letters.
The colonial leaders decided to unite in their cause.

5 THE BOSTON MASSACRE

On the evening of March 5, 1770, Crispus was in Boston. A colonist had done some work for a British soldier that night. The soldier refused to pay him. Quickly, news spread through Boston of this injustice. Colonists gathered in the streets. They yelled and threw snowballs and rocks at the British soldiers. The soldiers fought back.

PLUNDERING SOLDIERS.

British soldiers did many bad things that angered the colonists. This woodcut shows soldiers stealing from a colonist's home.

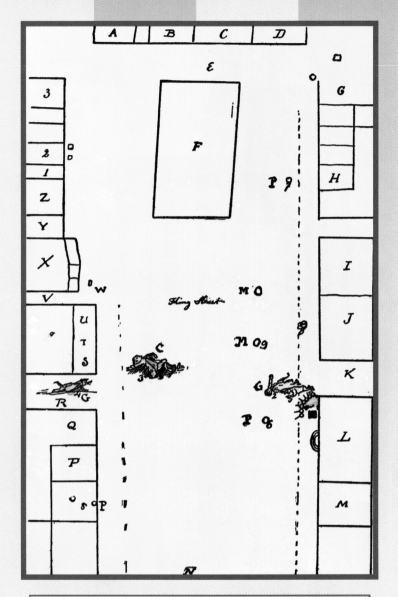

Paul Revere drew this map of the Boston Massacre site. He used letters and numbers to place people. King Street was crowded that March night. The fighting colonists and British soldiers were close to each other.

The soldiers hit colonists with sticks and the tips of their muskets. Crispus bravely joined his fellow colonists. He did not care about the color of their skin. The fight for freedom was more important to him. A big fight broke out on King Street in front of the Customs House. Crispus tried to grab a musket from one of the soldiers.

No one knows who fired the first shot at the Boston Massacre. This drawing shows the British soldiers firing upon the fleeing colonists.

Another drawing of the Boston Massacre shows a larger crowd. Here almost all of the British soldiers *(left side)* are firing into the crowd. Crispus Attucks was one of the first to die.

A British soldier shot and killed Crispus. Four other colonists were killed that night. Crispus Attucks was one of the first people to give his life for American independence. The Boston Massacre led to the Revolutionary War. The colonists won the war and became independent from Britain's rule. Crispus gave his life to help free the very colonists who once enslaved him.

DID YOU KNOW?

Crispus never married or had children.

Hours to the Gates of this City many Thousands of our brave Brethren in the Country, deeply affected with our Distresses, and to whom we are greatly obliged on this Occasion—No one knows where this would have ended, and what important Consequences even to the whole British Empire might have followed, which our Moderation & Loyalty upon so trying an Occasion, and our Faith in the Commander's Assurances have happily prevented.

Last Thursday, agreeable to a general Request of the Inhabitants, and by the Consent of Parents and Friends, were carried to their *Grave* in Succession, the Bodies of *Samuel Gray, Samuel Maverick, James Caldwell,* and *Crispus Attucks,* the unhappy Victims who fell in the bloody Massacre of the Monday Evening preceeding !

On this Occasion most of the Shops in Town were shut, all the Bells were ordered to toll a solemn Peal, as were also those in the neighboring Towns of Charlestown Roxbury, &c. The Procession began to move between the Hours of 4 and 5 in the Afternoon ; two of the unfortunate Sufferers, viz. Mess. *James Caldwell* and *Crispus Attucks,* who were Strangers, borne from Faneuil-Hall,

Colonial newspapers wrote about the five dead men from the Boston Massacre. The drawings of four of the coffins have the men's initials. Colonists used the memories of the dead men as a way to unite.

TIMELINE

1723—Crispus Attucks is born. He and his family are slaves in Framingham, Massachusetts.

1750—Crispus runs away to become a sailor.

1750-1770—Crispus works on a whaling ship.

1770—Crispus is one of the first men killed in the fight for American independence. This event became known as the Boston Massacre.

GLOSSARY

announcement (uh-NOWNS-ment) Something that is stated officially or publicly.

courage (KUR-ij) Bravery or fearlessness.

dangerous (DAYN-jer-us) Likely to cause harm or injury; not safe; risky.

freedom (FREE-dum) The right to do and say what one wants.

independence (in-dih-PEN-dents) Freedom from the control of others.

injustice (in-JUS-tis) An unfair act.

musket (MUHS-kit) A gun with a long barrel that was used before the rifle was invented.

slavery (SLAY-vuh-ree) When someone is owned by another person and thought of as property.

stray (STRAY) To wander away or get lost.

WEB SITES

Due to the changing nature of Internet links, the Rosen Publishing Group, Inc., has developed an online list of Web sites related to the subject of this book. This site is updated regularly. Please use this link to access the list:

http://www.rosenlinks.com/fpah/catt

PRIMARY SOURCE IMAGE LIST

Page 5: Illustrated portrait of Crispus Attucks, circa 1750.

Page 7: Color lithograph of Boston by Jacques Milbert. It is currently housed at the New York Historical Society, New York City.

Page 8: Illustration of seaman, 1777.

Page 9: An 1824 oil painting titled *A Pennsylvania County Fair* by John Archibald Woodside.

Page 10: An 1859 oil painting titled *Whaler Off the Vineyard* by William Bradford. It is currently housed at the Smithsonian American Art Museum, Washington, D.C.

Page 11: An illustration of a whaler stripping blubber from a catch.

Page 13: Color lithograph circa 1850 titled *American Whaler* by Nathaniel Currier. It is currently housed at the Yale University Art Gallery, New Haven, CT.

Page 14: An oil painting circa 1862 titled *A Ride for Liberty—The Fugitive Slaves* by Eastman Johnson. It is currently housed at the Brooklyn Museum of Art, Brooklyn, NY.

Page 17: Color engraving of whaling implements, circa second half of 18th century, by French School.

Page 19: An oil painting circa 1850 titled *A Whaling Scene* by Cornelius Krieghoff.

Page 20: Oil painting of King George III of England, 1760, by Allan Ramsay. It is currently housed at the Chateaux de Versailles et de Trianon, Versailles, France.
Page 21: Illustration titled *Stamp Act Protest*, 1765.
Page 23: An engraving circa 1774 titled *The First Continental Congress* by Francoise Godefroy.
Page 25: Paul Revere's hand-drawn plan of King Street in 1770.
Page 26: An illustration titled *Boston Massacre* appearing in *Harper's Weekly*, 1883. It is currently housed at the New York Public Library.
Page 27: Illustration titled *Death of Crispus Attucks* circa 1770s. It is currently housed at the New York Public Library.
Page 29: Printed obituaries of Crispus Attucks and others of the Boston Massacre, with engravings of four coffins bearing initials of the dead, by Paul Revere, 1770.

INDEX

ABOUT THE AUTHOR

Anne Beier writes children's books, and teaches creative writing and art for children at the NWCA. Anne lives with her husband and cat in Ossining, New York.